AWAKENED

When Success No Longer Feels Enough

EAST AWAKENER

This is not a book. It's a threshold.

For those no longer seeking more,
but ready to surrender deeper.

These are not teachings.
They are echoes—
reminders of the truth you carried in silence.

The world called it success.
The soul called it collapse.

This is the return.

Legal Notice:

Disclaimer Notice:

CONTENTS

INTRODUCTION :
THE UNEXPECTED AWAKENING

There is a moment in every soul's journey when the facade of external success can no longer be sustained. When the meticulously constructed edifice of achievement, professional recognition, and societal validation begins to crack, revealing the hollowness within. My moment arrived with unmistakable clarity on September 7, 2023, a night that decisively divided my life into "before" and "after."

I didn't set out on a journey to 'awaken.' In fact, I had never even heard of spiritual awakening. As a respected orthodontist with a thriving practice in Taiwan and an entrepreneur developing innovative products, I had deliberately built the life I thought I wanted. I had checked every box society told me would lead to fulfillment, professional credentials, business success, and international recognition.

And yet, beneath the polished veneer of my life, I was drowning.

The relentless pursuit of perfection, the exhaustion of constant striving, and the emptiness that no amount of travel, acquisition, or recognition could fill—these had become my constant companions. One of my favorite quotes pierced through my reality: "Many people are so poor, all they have is money." This was me. Materially abundant, spiritually bankrupt. Despite my outward accomplishments, I was inwardly disconnected from my true self.

With nowhere else to turn, I decided to seek comfort in faith. I began reading the Bible, worshiping sincerely, and simply praying to become a vessel God could use. At first, I was skeptical when people shared the gospel with me. But over time, I witnessed for myself that God is real. And yet, through all my years in church, no one ever spoke of awakening; it came as a surprise, a grace I never expected.

The night that transformed everything found me at a strategic breaking point. For three weeks leading up to my product launch on Amazon in the U.S., I had been wrestling with an overwhelming sense of failure. What should have been a crowning achievement in my entrepreneurial journey had become a source of crushing anxiety.

Production delays, quality control issues, and unexpected costs had strained my resources to the breaking point. Despite my outward competence, I felt myself coming undone from within. The carefully constructed identity I had built was crumbling, and for the first time, I could not devise a strategy to fix it.

And then, something powerful intervened. In that liminal space between consciousness and sleep, my soul separated from my body. I heard myself speak with unexpected authority and clarity:

"(My Name), what are you doing? Can't you see you're an amazing person?"

When I awoke the next morning, everything had fundamentally shifted.

I was filled with a peace and joy I had never experienced before, not the manufactured happiness I had trained myself to project, but a profound sense of wholeness radiating from my core. Suddenly, I felt powerfully connected to everything—people, animals, and plants. Most remarkably, the questions and problems that had consumed me seemed to dissolve overnight.

As my therapist later explained, what I had experienced was a spiritual awakening. This is not a story of a "chosen one" or someone with special abilities. I am not writing from some elevated plane untouched by real-world demands. I was born into an ordinary family. I built a conventional professional practice. I navigated the challenges of leading a business, creating a meaningful family life, and searching for purpose, just as you may be doing now.

What differentiates this journey is not who I am, but what awakened within me and what can awaken within you. The divine connection that reignited in my soul exists within each person reading these words, regardless of your background, beliefs, or current circumstances.

My awakening path took me from the structured world of dentistry to the unpredictable domain of entrepreneurship, from the familiar environment of Taiwan to the sacred heights of the Himalayas. Through this transformation, I discovered that spiritual awakening isn't about escaping our human experience but about engaging it fully, with new perspectives and an awakened heart.

A DIVINE CALLING

This book was conceived during a meditation in May 2024, nine months after that night in September. In that moment of stillness, I saw myself clearly: Standing confidently at the head of a long wooden table, surrounded by books I had written. I knew in that instant that this wasn't just about me anymore.

God spoke to me. And I don't say that lightly. He didn't ask something *from* me; He offered something *to* all of us. The message was simple and piercing:

He wants to connect with everyone. But that connection requires that we first wake up.

Created in His Image

Even now, writing this, the tears come back. That moment was more real than anything I'd ever experienced. It was beyond logic, beyond words. That's when I knew, I had to write this book.

"So God created mankind in His own image."

That's not a poetic metaphor. It's a direct reminder that the divine is already within you.

This isn't a mystical prize for the elite. It's your birthright. But we only *see* it once we awaken.

Why "East Awakener?"

I write under the name "East Awakener" not to create distance but to emphasize that this message transcends individual identity. The awakening matters more than the messenger. This approach allows me to share my journey authentically while maintaining focus on the universal invitation to awakening that extends to all who have achieved external success but hunger for internal alignment.

INTEGRATIVE SPIRITUALITY

My spiritual journey integrates Christian worship, prayer, and Bible study with the meditation practices I discovered after my awakening. This path doesn't conform neatly to traditional Christianity or New Age philosophy. Instead, it represents what I call Integrative Spirituality—a personal, sacred synthesis of Christian faith and Eastern practices that deepened my experience of connecting with the Divine in daily life.

Whether you picked up this book as a successful professional wondering why the emptiness won't go away, an entrepreneur craving deeper meaning, a Christian longing for a more intimate relationship with God, or simply someone quietly wrestling with the space between who you are and who you *feel* you're meant to be, there's something here for you.

You'll walk with me through a deeply personal awakening that began not in struggle, but in the peak of external success. I wasn't searching for a spiritual experience. Life looked great on paper. I was an orthodontist turned entrepreneur, having built the MINIBOX Toothbrush brand. I was working hard, mentoring others, and growing the business. And yet underneath all that motion, something holy and unsettling stirred, a quiet discontent I couldn't shake.

From Achievement to Alignment

Then came the awakening. Sudden. Unexpected. Unmistakable. And it turned everything upside down, in the best way. It changed how I viewed my work, my family, my ambition, and my relationship with God. What once felt like pressure and performance began to feel like purpose and alignment. My business, of all things, became sacred ground. I stopped chasing outcomes and started listening for divine direction in everyday choices.

This book is for anyone going through that in-between space: You are having everything together on the outside and feeling out of sync inside. You believe in God but feel disconnected. You've checked every box, yet something's still missing. Through ten raw and honest chapters, I'll share how this awakening reshaped not just my beliefs, but how I live, lead, and love.

You'll learn how to:

- Recognize God's voice beyond your own thoughts.
- Face fear without losing your center.
- Stop striving and start surrendering, without giving up your vision.
- Weave spiritual awareness into your work, relationships, and daily rhythm.
- Live with peace, purpose, and a steady connection to God.

This is for the ones who look accomplished but feel like something's missing.

It's for high achievers, ambitious believers, creative thinkers, and curious souls who know there's more but don't want to abandon what they've built to find it.

An Invitation to Awaken

This isn't just about having a spiritual awakening. It's about learning how to *walk with God* in the middle of your everyday life. Through prayer, Scripture, worship, and stillness, not as rituals, but as lifelines. It's about letting that connection reshape how you live and what you live for.

My journey, from a fragmented life as a dentist and entrepreneur to a more integrated, spiritually awake life, wasn't just mine. It opened up a path that I believe is available to anyone. This book invites you to look past the titles, roles, and expectations that may have defined your life and remember who you truly are.

If you're reading this, it's probably because something has already begun to stir inside you.
A quiet shift. A sense that the life you've built is no longer enough.
Not because you've failed—but because a deeper part of you is ready to awaken.

This book isn't about me.
It's about you.
Not the you the world sees, but the one God originally designed.

The one buried beneath roles, expectations, performance, and pain.
The one waiting to be realigned with something sacred and real.

I'm not here to inspire you to become more.
I'm here to remind you of who you already are.
And to call you back—to the voice within, to the truth you've always carried,
to the purpose that God whispered into your soul long before the world named you.

This is my offering.
Not a guidebook, but a mirror.
Not a conclusion, but an invitation.

The awakening has already begun.
The only question is:
Will you answer it? Will you live for what you were born for?

CHAPTER 7:

OBSTACLES TO AWAKENING—
LESSONS BEFORE SPIRITUAL AWAKENING—
OVERCOMING ANGER, FORGIVENESS, SUBMISSION,
HUMILITY, AND THE CHANGES AFTER AWAKENING

Overcoming Anger

One of my biggest struggles during the years when I seemed to have it all together—a successful clinic, a steady income, and respect from others—was my anger. Not just irritation. Not mood swings. I'm talking about full-on rage. Explosions. Sometimes two or three times a day, over things that didn't even matter. It was like I was a pressure cooker, and any little thing could push me over the edge.

I remember one moment clearly: After snapping at someone again, I just stood there, breathless and ashamed. And a verse from one of our Bible study sessions floated back to me:

"In your anger, do not sin. Do not let the sun go down while you are still angry..."

And I realized I had been letting the sun go down angry for years. I wasn't just dealing with a bad habit. It was about something I had buried deep inside.

Another verse echoed later:

"Whoever is patient has great understanding, but the one who is quick-tempered displays folly."

I didn't feel wise. I felt tired. Drained. Ashamed. And somehow... still unable to stop. I even kept a journal for a year, tracking every outburst, the triggers, the time of day, and the fallout. I was desperate to break the cycle, but no matter how hard I tried to manage it, nothing changed.

Looking back, I can see now: It wasn't just about self-control. It was about control, period. My obsession with perfection. My fear of falling short. My refusal to let go of expectations, of others, of myself, of life. And beneath all of it... was pain I hadn't yet faced.

Something beautiful happened when I first began to explore faith. You know how sometimes people jokingly make these deals with God? At that time, although I had already been baptized, I didn't truly believe in God. So I secretly tried to make a deal with Him. I said,

"God, if You can help me fix my temper, then I'll believe in You."

And you know what happened? When something aligns with God's will, He always makes it happen. The moment that changed everything is burned into my memory forever. I was right there on the edge of one of my classic explosions, mouth open, ready to unleash on someone, when suddenly, and I mean suddenly, the Holy Spirit flooded my mind with the most incredible clarity.

It was like a mirror being held up to my soul, and I saw all my flaws and imperfections. But he still loved me. In that moment, I realized, if He could love someone as imperfect as me, how could I stay angry at someone else when I myself had been shown such mercy? In that instant, my anger just... dissolved.

Vanished. Like it had never been there at all.

After that moment, my temper began to improve dramatically. You've probably heard people say that real change can't come from human effort alone; it has to be through the Holy Spirit's power. I used to think that was just nice religious talk, but now I know it's the deepest truth. That's also the first time I witnessed God's power.

Some people say they pray when they're angry, but honestly? When you're in the heat of that rage, you can barely think straight, let alone pray. Now, whenever I feel that familiar heat rising in my chest, instead of reacting right away, I've learned to take a breath, walk away if I need to, and ask God silently:

"What's really going on inside me?"

Later, when I've calmed down, I write about it to understand the deeper reasons behind the anger, whether it's pride, fear, or hurt.

As I began examining the roots of my anger, something amazing happened: I got faster at recognizing the real reasons behind it. And before I could even open my mouth to say something I'd regret, the anger would just... leave.

How I View Anger After Awakening

Learning to control anger is absolutely essential before you can experience true spiritual awakening. We have to become more like God to reach that place, at least, that's how I understand it.

By the time awakening came, I had already learned to manage my temper pretty well. From exploding multiple times a day, I was down to maybe once or twice a year. But let me tell you how everything changed after awakening.

We live in a world where emotions are unavoidable, especially when you have a strong sense of justice like I do. I still see unfair, imperfect things happening at work and everywhere else; they're always there. So how do you face these things after awakening?

Here's what I've come to understand: not all emotions are wrong. Righteous anger has its place, especially in a world where injustice exists. We are not called to be numb. But what transforms a moment is how we respond. When you react emotionally to something, you become entangled in the world's chaos and absorb all that toxic energy, and that's dangerous territory. Negative energy calls to more negative energy like a magnet. After awakening, I understood that avoiding emotional reactions isn't just wise, it's essential. Because when you react, you're basically sending out an invitation for more of that energy to flood your life, and it can grow into something completely uncontrollable.

When we feel anger, we can choose to pause, to process, and to invite God into that space.

When we respond from a place of grounded peace rather than reactive rage, we create room for divine justice to unfold. Sometimes, what we think requires our force, God resolves in far greater ways than we could ever orchestrate.

The most incredible realization is that anger itself can be a test, not one to suppress, but one to observe with spiritual clarity. Not all anger is wrong. In fact, righteous anger is often a response to real injustice in the world. But the deeper invitation is this: how will you respond? When we treat anger like a passing breeze, acknowledging it without being consumed by it, we create space for God to act.

Often, what seemed urgent or offensive either resolves on its own or loses its grip on us. There's no need to waste our precious energy fighting every battle, because God is already moving on our behalf. I know this may sound hard to believe, but try it. Trust Him. Pause. And experience what happens when you don't let anger lead but let peace remain.

Key Takeaways

- Anger and temper can absolutely be overcome, but not through willpower alone; it has to be through God's strength.

- Study the roots of your anger. Ask yourself, *wWhy am I really upset?* Let this self-discovery help you grow closer to God's heart.

- In the heat of the moment, choose stillness over reaction. Most reactions only escalate the situation. When you pause and let God lead, even "impossible" conflicts can dissolve.

- Never underestimate the spiritual impact of unresolved anger. Anger isn't just a personality flaw; it can block intimacy with God, distort your decisions, and delay your calling.

FORGIVENESS

Forgiveness isn't a one-time lesson; it's a lifelong path. At different points in our lives, we'll be invited to forgive all kinds of people: our parents, our partners, our children, friends, coworkers, and even strangers who hurt us deeply and unfairly.

One of the hardest lessons I ever faced came during a season when I felt completely misunderstood and betrayed. I had tried to stand for what was right, to speak up for justice, but instead of being supported, I was judged, dismissed, and isolated.

There were days I cried out to God, asking:

"Why does doing the right thing hurt so much?"

And then, in the quiet of my soul, I heard Him speak:

"I love the world."

At first, I didn't understand. But slowly, it became clear: God doesn't only love us when we're right. He also loves the people we think are wrong. That truth was hard to accept, but it set me free. I realized that even when I am hurt, God's love is still big enough to hold everyone involved. His justice is not like human judgment. His mercy is not selective.

So I chose to forgive. Not because it was easy or because they deserved it, but because I didn't want bitterness to grow where peace was meant to live. I even began to pray for them, tearfully, honestly, because I realized they too are beloved by God.

"Love your enemies and pray for those who persecute you... that you may be children of your Father in heaven."

It might feel impossible at first, but when you forgive from the heart, you begin to taste the freedom only God can give.

Forgiveness After Awakening

After awakening, I came to see that everything happening to us is woven into God's beautiful plan. Forgiveness becomes a test, and each time you pass it, you move closer to spiritual awakening.

SUBMISSION

One of the most profound lessons I ever learned about submission came during those nine long years I spent developing my product. At one point, the delays and setbacks wore me down so deeply, I didn't want to keep going. I just wanted to walk away and help others in my own way. So I did. I started organizing gatherings for young entrepreneurs, offering advice and encouragement to anyone who asked. I threw myself into charitable giving. I gave generously to those in need—meals, clean water, shoes, whatever I could. But deep inside, there was a growing ache.

It wasn't that giving was wrong. I knew those acts mattered. But something in me kept crying out to God:

"Anyone with money and supplies can donate things. But You gave me a different kind of gift, one that comes from pain, from process. Is this all my gifts are meant for? Just give things away?"

That silent cry wasn't just frustration; it was grief. Grief for the dream I had once held so purely: the desire to help people, not just with things, but with the unique gift You had placed within me. I brought all of this to God in prayer. I told Him I didn't understand. I was trying to do good. I was trying to be useful. And then He told me something that shattered me:

"Close your mouth, and stop trying to help the entrepreneurs you believe you're meant to help."

I was devastated. Heartbroken. I remember sitting there, stunned, thinking:

"How can wanting to help people possibly be wrong?"

But God lovingly told me to focus on finishing my product first. So I submitted to His will and stopped talking about helping entrepreneurs, even though it felt like I was abandoning my calling. I had no idea that through my submission, God was preparing me for something infinitely bigger. It wasn't a rebuke; it was a redirection. A call to surrender my ideas of how I should serve and trust that His way of using me would come not through my efforts but through obedience.

I had always thought I was ready, but God was refining me into a qualified entrepreneur. Now I can tackle challenges I never could have handled before, and my ability to guide others has grown beyond what I ever imagined. Submission was the key that unlocked God's greater plan for my life, and that's why I'm able to share this story with you in this book today.

Submission After Awakening

After awakening, submission became effortless. I didn't need to force myself anymore; I simply trusted God's plan completely. Even things that seemed utterly impossible became achievable through submission. This very book you're reading is a fruit of that surrender.

HUMILITY

Humility completely transformed how I related to my employees. I used to think, "I'm the boss. I sign the paychecks. They should respect me and see me as their superior." But after God taught me about true humility, I realized that every single person is equally precious in His eyes.

I used to scoff at the whole idea of "servant leadership," thinking, "How can I, the one paying all the bills, be expected to serve my employees?" But then I began to understand what real leadership looks like in God's kingdom.

Even the One who was divine in nature did not cling to His status or use it for personal advantage. Instead, He chose to let it go— to take on the form of a servant, to live as one of us, and to humble Himself to the point of ultimate sacrifice. And it was precisely because He lowered Himself that He was lifted up.

That changed everything for me. I realized that humility isn't weakness—it's strength under surrender. When you approach leadership this way, your employees will look up to you not because of your position, but because of your presence. Not because you pay their salaries, but because you live with honor. Those who try to exalt themselves may eventually fall—but those who choose humility will, in time, be lifted up.

Humility After Awakening

After awakening, humility became even more profound. You feel this incredible connection to everything—God, the universe, all of nature—and you realize just how small we really are in the grand scheme of things. How could we possibly be anything but humble?

GLOSSARY

- *Alignment: The state of harmony between awakened awareness and its expression through daily activities, decisions, and relationships; integration of spiritual recognition with practical engagement*

- *Awakening: The fundamental shift in perspective where consciousness recognizes its own nature beyond identification with temporary thoughts, emotions, and sensations; a recognition of what already exists rather than achievement of something new.*

- *East Awakener: The author's pen name, reflecting both geographical origin in Taiwan (East) and spiritual function as one who has awakened and shares this possibility with others.*

- *Fear: The emotional response arising from perceived threats to physical safety, psychological security, or identity maintenance; significantly diminished after awakening through recognition that fundamental awareness remains unchanged regardless of temporary circumstances.*

- *Identity: The sense of self constructed through identification with particular roles, achievements, characteristics, and experiences; recognized as useful but limited construction after awakening rather than fundamental reality.*

- *MINIBOX: The travel toothbrush brand developed by the author during a nine-year journey that paralleled her spiritual transformation; a physical manifestation of purpose beyond profit.*

- *Meditation: The practice of directing attention toward awareness itself rather than exclusively focusing on thought content; a method for recognizing consciousness beyond thinking.*

- *Purpose: The authentic expression of consciousness through individual gifts and circumstances beyond egoic achievement or social expectations; what genuinely matters beyond conditioned patterns.*

- *Recognition: The direct perception of what already exists rather than achievement of something new; the primary mode of awakening as distinguished from accomplishment or acquisition.*

- *Surrender: Releasing attachment to specific outcomes while maintaining appropriate engagement; not passive resignation but active allowing without unnecessary resistance or control.*

- *Thought: Mental activity including concepts, judgments, memories, plans, and self-references; recognized after awakening as appearance within consciousness rather than defining reality or identity.*

The Bible verses quoted in this book are not included for religious instruction, but rather as part of my own soul's awakening journey. These words were the light, comfort, and divine guidance I personally received in my darkest hours.

I am not a pastor, a theologian, or a representative of any church or denomination. These verses are a reflection of my personal connection with God, not a doctrine I expect others to adopt.

If you are a Christian, I invite you to listen again for the gentle and true voice behind these words. If you come from a different faith background, I ask you to read these verses as poetic fragments from a soul in transformation.

This is not about asking you to convert. It is an invitation to remember that you too have a soul journey, and that there is a Creator who knows you, sees you, and is patiently waiting for you to hear His voice.

Printed in Dunstable, United Kingdom